Dance Style File

Written and arranged for keyboards
by Adrian York

QUICKSTEP	Fly Me To The Moon	3
JUMP/JIVE	Is You Is, Or Is You Ain't (Ma' Baby)	6
BOSSANOVA	The Girl From Ipanema	10
REGGAE	No Woman, No Cry	14
HIP-HOP	Killing Me Softly With His Song	18
HOUSE	Missing	22
RHYTHM & BLUES	I Got You (I Feel Good)	26
GARAGE	Where Love Lives	30
SWINGBEAT	My Prerogative	34
CALYPSO/SOCA	Hot, Hot, Hot	38
ACID JAZZ	Apparently Nothin'	42
FUNK	Pick Up The Pieces	46
JAZZ-FUNK	Birdland	50
SALSA	Oye Mi Canto	55
DISCO	I Will Survive	60

Chester Music
(A division of Music Sales Limited)
8/9 Frith Street
London W1V 5TZ

Introduction

This series of three books (Jazz & Blues Style File, Pop & Rock Style File and Dance Style File) forms a collection of progressively graded arrangements of the best known tunes representing all the main pop styles, providing a core repertoire for popular music piano/keyboard studies.

Each arrangement is preceded by a set of notes that looks at the musical history, social background and musical make-up of the genre, emphasising the role of the musicians involved.

These books will be a useful resource for any pianists or piano teachers looking for a non-classical repertoire. As part of the style notes there are exercises which deal with many of the technical issues that are relevant to the non-classical musician such as playing with a convincing 'swing' feel (for both jazz and contemporary dance music), a solid approach to time-keeping, syncopation and rhythmic independence between the hands.

I hope you have as much fun using them as I have had putting them together.

Adrian York

This book © Copyright 1997 Chester Music
Order No. CH61278 ISBN 0-7119-6445-9

Music processed by Barnes Music Engraving.
Cover design by xheight design Limited.
Printed in Great Britain by
Printwise (Haverhill) Limited, Haverhill, Suffolk.

Unauthorised reproduction of any part of this publication by any means including photocopying is an infringement of copyright.

Quickstep Ballroom Dancing

It is hard to connect the highly disciplined and regulated world of ballroom dancing with the latest dance moves being seen at raves or clubs, or to believe that the music accompanying the moves could in its day have been as fashionable as contemporary sounds in dance music. In fact, the British dance band leaders of the late 1920s through to the 50s (such as Geraldo, Ambrose and Jack Hylton) were probably better known than any of those icons of the contemporary dance music scene, the DJs. In many ways fronting a dance band involves similar skills to DJing, as the aim is to control and keep the dance floor full by choosing material of an appropriate speed and rhythm.

The dances themselves come from a wide variety of cultural and social backgrounds but were standardised in 1924 by the Imperial Society of Teachers of Dancing (ISTD) and are now divided into two groups: standard dances (waltz, tango, Viennese waltz, slow foxtrot and quickstep) and Latin American dances (samba, cha-cha-cha, rumba, paso doble and jive). Whereas the contemporary DJ works with 'beats per minute' as their units for regulating tempo, ballroom dancing works with bars (units of four, or for waltzes, three beats) per minute, with the up tempo quickstep falling at 50 and the slower more sensuous rumba at 27. These tempi are strictly adhered to.

These dance styles had truly international and socially varied backgrounds. The English waltz derived from the American dance the 'Boston', which dated from the 1870s. The Viennese waltz traces its ancestry back to a 13th century German dance, the Nachtanz. The familiar Strauss melodies stem from the late 1700s, but even in the 1800s the waltz was considered 'a dance of too loose character for maidens to perform', felt to be safe only for married women. The tango, which came out of 'El Barria de las Ranas', the ghetto area in the Argentinian capital Buenos Aires, was based on the Spanish 'habanera' rhythm that so influenced the music of the birthplace of jazz, New Orleans. The tango was a source of great social alarm in its day, with French bishops condemning it for its sexual openness and the New York Times claiming in a 1915 headline that 'The Tango Danger Is Bigger Than German Imperialism'.

The Latin dances all have exciting backgrounds, the samba coming to Brazil via Africa and also providing the rhythms for the Cuban mambo, rumba and cha-cha. The paso doble was a Spanish dance from the 1920s which recreates the spirit of the bullfight with the male dancer representing the toreador and the female the red canvas that the toreador uses. The jive stemmed from the jitterbug, the dance step of choice in New York's Harlem with the swinging sounds of the big bands. The quickstep developed in the 1920s as bands played the foxtrot at faster paces, maybe influenced by uptempo dances such as the Charleston.

'Fly Me To The Moon', with its imagery of speeding through space, is a perfect choice for the effortless glide of the quickstep.

FLY ME TO THE MOON (IN OTHER WORDS)

Words & Music by Bart Howard

© Copyright 1954, 1962, 1973 by Almanac Music Incorporated, New York, USA.
Assigned to TRO Essex Music Limited, Suite 2.07, Plaza 535 Kings Road, London SW10 for the World (excluding Canada and USA).
All Rights Reserved. International Copyright Secured.

Jump/jive

Up to the early 1940s, jazz groups were employed as dance bands, whose musicians and singers provided mainstream entertainment. The band leaders and big band singers (including the young Frank Sinatra) were given pop star treatment, but there was a growing resentment amongst many black musicians about the racism, financial rip-offs and lack of credit for musical innovations that they encountered compared to their white counterparts.

A group of young black musicians in New York responded to these circumstances by developing a style of jazz named bebop, which turned the music away from the dance floor and popular entertainment, into something much more cerebral and difficult for a mass audience to grasp. This was a transition from popular to high art, and what is now known as 'modern jazz' has been institutionalised into the seats of learning of high culture: the universities, conservatories and concert halls.

However, whilst Charlie Parker and Dizzy Gillespie were forging ahead with the new musical ideas of bebop, another equally significant strand of black jazz-based music was making its presence felt. The jump bands of the early 1940s (to which people danced the jive) came from a tradition of popular black entertainment that goes back to the start of the 20th century (with the minstrel shows) and continues to the present day with hip-hop and swingbeat, and was also the basis for rock 'n' roll and all its offshoots.

Black stars were starting to become popular with white audiences throughout the 1930s, one of the most famous being the extraordinary entertainer, Cab Calloway. Calloway, with his famous 'hi-de-ho' catch phrase and white top hat, tails and cane was well-known for his exuberance on stage. He would sing and dance his way through songs such as 'Minnie The Moocher' and 'The Reefer Man', and he influenced the young Louis Jordan, an alto saxophonist and singer, who started his career in the Rabbit Foot Minstrels backing the legendary blues divas Ma Rainey and Bessie Smith.

In 1936 Jordan joined the well-known Chick Webb Orchestra where he outshone both the bandleader and the official band singer, Ella Fitzgerald. On Webb's death in 1938 Jordan formed his own band, The Tympany Five, and in 1939 he signed to Decca records, producing 19 hits in the 1944-49 period. These included 'Choo Choo Ch' Boogie', 'Ain't Nobody Here But Us Chickens', 'Caldonia', 'Saturday Night Fish Fry' and the million selling 'Is You Is, Or Is You Ain't Ma' Baby'. Jordan's record producer Milt Gabler went on to produce early white rock 'n' rollers Bill Haley And The Comets who strove to copy Jordan's sound on tracks like 'Rock Around The Clock'.

Try transposing this exercise into other keys. To get that authentic jump feel, make sure that your quavers (eighth notes) are placed somewhere between ♪♪♪ and ♪.♪

IS YOU IS, OR IS YOU AIN'T (MA' BABY)

Words & Music by Billy Austin & Louis Jordan

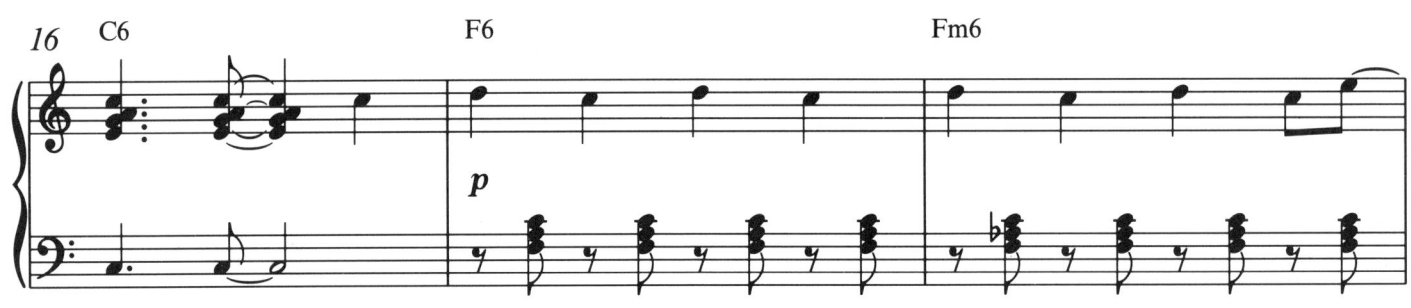

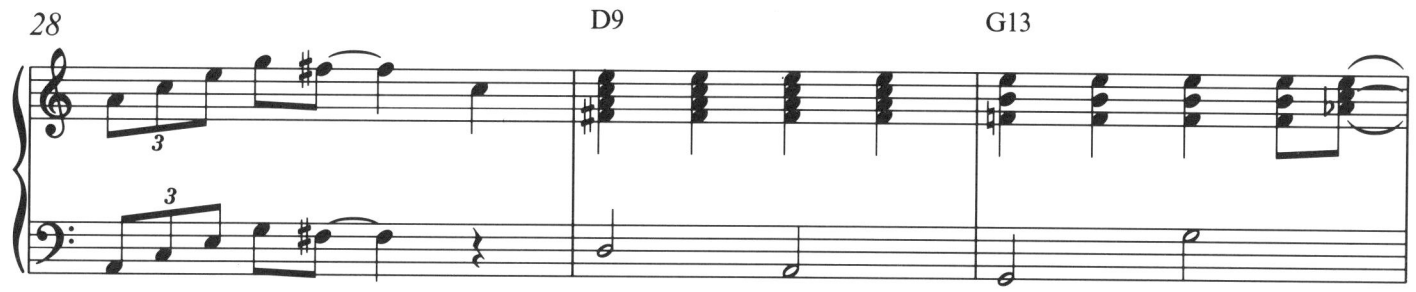

Bossanova

In Brazil (as in other Latin American countries) music, dancing and the culture of rhythm are essential components of everyday life. The collision of Spanish/Portuguese, Northern European and African influences created a vital and popular musical scene which has served as a breeding ground for new musical styles. The most important of these styles is the samba, which started as a folk rhythm played by country people in the hills of Bahia in northern Brazil. By the 1940s the samba was dominating the Brazilian musical scene and started to spread internationally. Composer Ary Barroso was the best known of the samba writers and his song 'Brazil' has been a hit worldwide many times over.

By the late 1950s a new generation of Brazilian musicians came to the fore. They were mostly from European backgrounds, middle-class, educated and schooled in American jazz and the harmonic construction of jazz standards (songs from films and shows by writers such as George and Ira Gershwin, Rodgers and Hart and Cole Porter). West Coast 'cool' jazz of artists such as pianist Dave Brubeck, saxophonists Stan Getz and Art Pepper and trumpeter Chet Baker made a big impression on young Brazilian musicians such as guitarist Joao Gilberto.

Gilberto along with his friend Antonio Carlos Jobim brought together a slowed down samba rhythm, the cool jazz feel and the chords used in the jazz standards to create a new hybrid: the bossanova ('new beat'). Gilberto started recording bossanovas in 1958 with Jobim becoming the leading writer in the genre. Tunes such as 'Corcovado', 'Desafinado' and 'One Note Samba' were all given English lyrics and became popular internationally, with artists such as Frank Sinatra, Miles Davis and Ella Fitzgerald covering Jobim's material.

The bossanova boom reached its peak in 1964 with the release of what became Jobim's best known song, 'The Girl From Ipanema'. The English version, featuring Jobim himself on guitar, the cool tenor saxophone of Stan Getz and the beguiling voice of Astrud Gilberto offered the world a glimpse of a sophisticated and sensuous Brazil.

Classic bossanova feel:

THE GIRL FROM IPANEMA
(GAROTA DE IPANEMA)

Original Words by Vinicius De Moraes
English Lyric by Norman Gimbel
Music by Antonio Carlos Jobim

Medium Latin ♩ = 106

© Copyright 1963 Antonio Carlos Jobim and Vinicius De Moraes, Brazil.
MCA Music Limited, 77 Fulham Palace Road, London W6 for the British Commonwealth
(excluding Canada) South Africa, Eire, Germany, Austria, Switzerland, France and Italy.
All Rights Reserved. International Copyright Secured.

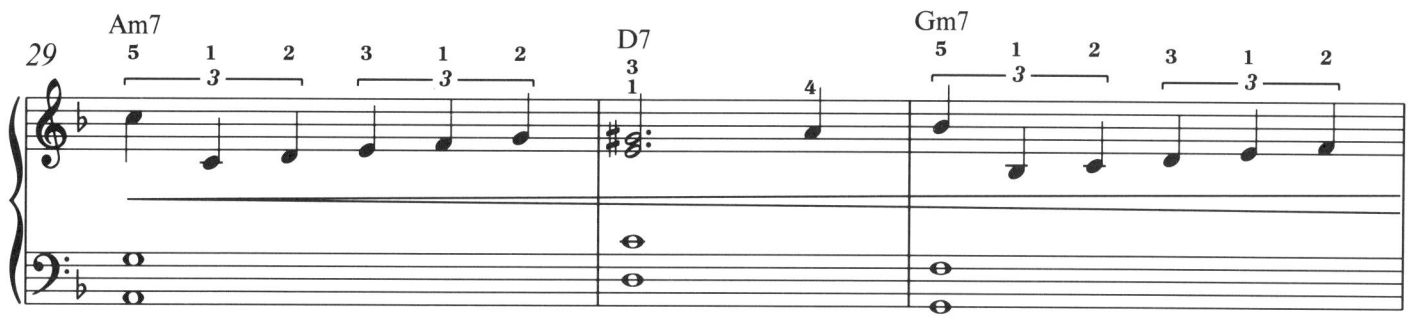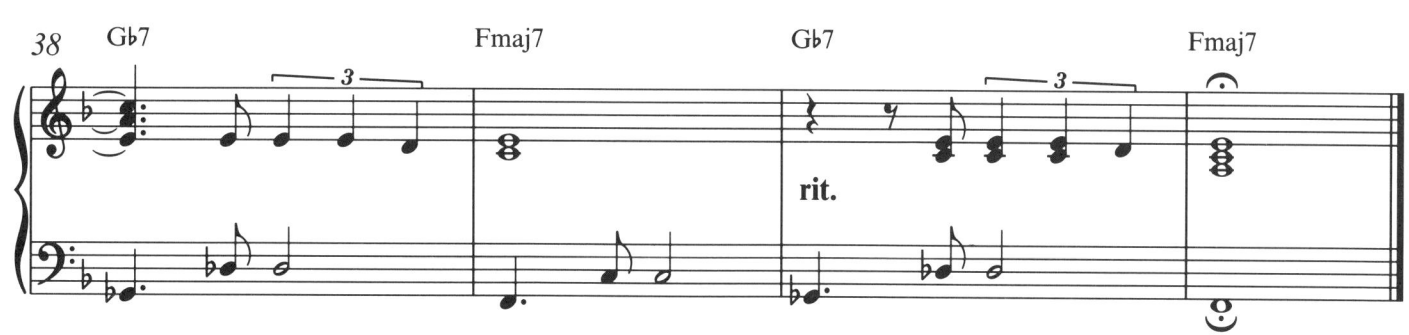

Reggae

The roots of reggae are to be found in the loosely structured Jamaican folk song form of 'mento'. Mento sounded similar to the Trinidadian form of calypso, and its lyrical content addressed the topical issues of the day. Mento declined in popularity in Jamaica during the 1950s as American rhythm and blues became immensely popular, promoted by radio stations and the growth in dance hall sound systems (early discotheques). The decline of rhythm and blues and rock 'n' roll in the early 1960s created a gap in the market for up tempo dance music which was filled by the development of 'ska'. This was a hybrid of New Orleans rhythm and blues and mento rhythms, featuring the distinctive piano or guitar 'chop' on the second and fourth beats.

The first ska tune to be recorded was Theophilous Beckford's 'Easy Snapping' of 1959 and sound systems such as Sir Coxsone's Downbeat were happy to have local material to promote. Musicians involved in the scene, such as Ernest Ranglin and the original line-up of the Skatalites, one of the best known ska acts, were often accomplished jazz musicians. As the 1960s progressed the tempo of ska slowed down but the social commentary present in mento appeared again, with artists like Prince Buster gaining a large street gang 'rude boy' following. It was this aspect of ska that influenced British groups such as The Specials, Selecter and Madness in the ska revival of the late 1970s.

As the tempo slowed further, the more sophisticated sound of 'rocksteady' developed. Named after the Alton Ellis hit 'Get Ready To Rocksteady', this sensuous sound emphasised the bass on beats one and three (taking over from the drums as the main rhythmic impetus) with the piano or guitar on the second and fourth.

Jamaican music had begun to attract international attention in the 1960s with releases coming from white Jamaican Chris Blackwell's London based Island Records. From early releases such as Millie Small's 'My Boy Lollipop' onwards (which reached no.2 in the American charts in 1964) Blackwell was committed to promoting Jamaican music internationally. In 1972 he recorded the first major album, 'Catch A Fire' by Bob Marley And The Wailers. The rocksteady beat had slowed down to a mesmerising bump and grind and the inspiration for Marley's songs was fuelled by his Rastafarian beliefs and his love of ganja (marijuana).

This was the formula which propelled the reggae sound of his third album, the 1975 release 'Natty Dread', to the forefront of hip white liberal consciousness. The song from this album, 'No Woman No Cry', features the beautiful organ work of Bernard 'Touter' Harvey, who gives us all an object lesson in the subtle art of playing the Hammond Organ. He adds an incredible warmth to the track whilst simultaneously creating beautiful countermelodies to add a spiritual quality to the music.

Marley went on to international superstardom but died a premature death of cancer in 1981. His music and son Ziggy are his legacy and he has become a symbol of Jamaica and its culture.

Practise the reggae offbeat 'chop' at a slow tempo and with a metronome: it can be quite hard to place it accurately.

NO WOMAN, NO CRY

Words & Music by Bob Marley & Vincent Ford

Hip-hop

The story of hip-hop culture is a classic example of how a localised scene (from the South Bronx) exploded worldwide to become a dominant force in popular culture. The word 'hip-hop' itself is generally credited with having been brought into use in the late 1970s by one of the earliest rapping DJs, DJ Hollywood. He used the phrase as a basis for creating rhythmic, verbal rhymes and improvisations which he would half talk/half sing ('rap') over funky disco tracks.

Hip-hop became a catch-all word encompassing the many different elements of the South Bronx street culture. These elements included graffiti art and breakdancing, an athletic and rhythmic form of dancing often performed on street corners. Another aspect was DJing and MCing (MC stands for master of ceremonies and refers to the rappers). The second wave of DJs such as Grandmaster Flash developed innovative techniques: cutting between one record and another at incredible speed, and manipulating the record deck to create a rhythmic 'scratching' effect. MCs and DJs formed themselves into 'crews' to perform: normally two DJs and five MCs, with one MC being assigned the job of 'beatboxing', creating a funky percussive beat with their voice and body for the other MCs to rap over.

The roots of rap itself stems from Afro-American and African culture. Much of what is termed hardcore rap presents an alternative urban oral history which can be traced back through early rural blues musicians to the oral historians of the great West African tribes, the Griots. The first rap breakthrough hit record was released in 1979: 'Rapper's Delight' by the Sugarhill Gang. The DJ skills of scratching and mixing together different backing tracks to create something new were featured in Grandmaster Flash's 'Wheels Of Steel', based on samples of recordings by Queen, Chic and Blondie.

The successful artists in the first few years of recorded hip-hop principally made party records and are now termed 'old school'. There was a change in mood in 1982 with the release of the Grandmaster Flash album, 'The Message', which dealt in violent social imagery and comment as well as urban paranoia: with the lead track featuring the classic couplet 'Don't push me, 'cos I'm close to the edge'. This new, aggressive hardcore style of hip-hop became epitomised by the work of Public Enemy and Run DMC. Run DMC were two rappers and a DJ whose third album ('Raisin' Hell', released in 1986) was the first hip-hop album to achieve platinum status. They also crashed into the pop charts and onto MTV in the same year with their version of heavy rockers Aerosmith's 'Walk This Way'.

Hip-hop spread outwards from New York, giving credibility to lightweight pop styles, and fusing with jazz and also Jamaican dancehall music (to create 'ragga') on its way. Meanwhile, the next stylistic twist was taking place in the black ganglands of Los Angeles. In 1988 Niggaz With Attitude released 'Straight Outta Compton', a celebration of the violence and lifestyle of Los Angeles' gang members which initiated the highly commercial 'gangsta' rap style. This was continued by artists such as Ice Cube, Ice T, Snoop Doggy Dog and Tupac Shakur.

The mid 1990s has seen the rise of The Fugees, whose soulful brand of hip-hop has a cinematic sense of imagery and has been used in many film soundtracks. Their version of the classic Roberta Flack hit of the 1970s with its 'one time' hook line was a huge international hit, establishing them as the leading pop/hip-hop artists of their time.

A typical repetitive hip-hop groove. Because much hip-hop is based on samples, the music tends to repeat sections over and over again, just as funk artists did in the 1960s. Remember to swing the semiquavers (sixteenth notes) in hip-hop.

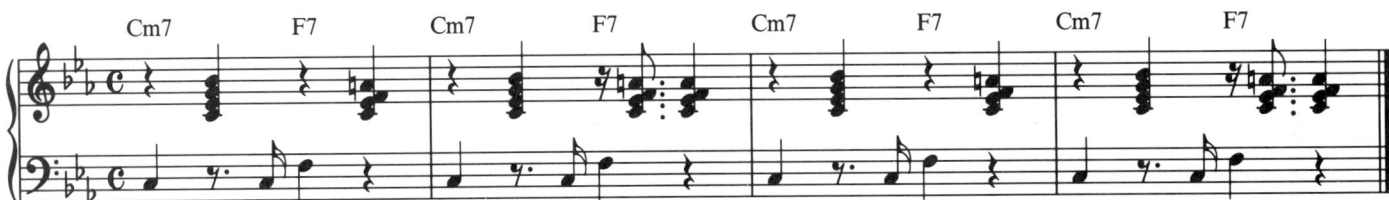

KILLING ME SOFTLY WITH HIS SONG

Words by Norman Gimbel
Music by Charles Fox

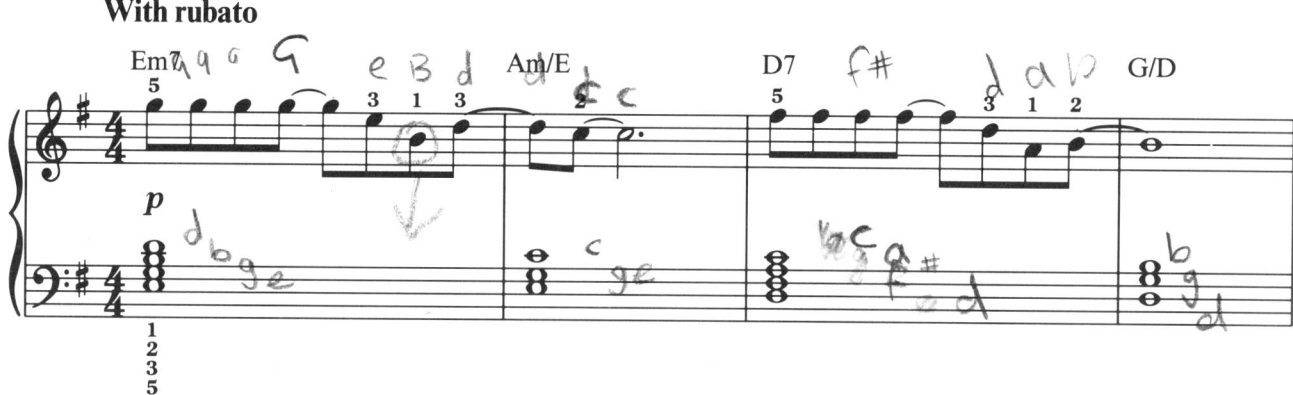

© Copyright 1972 Fox-Gimbel Productions Incorporated, USA.
Assigned to Onward Music Limited, 11 Uxbridge Street, London W8 for the British Commonwealth
(excluding Canada), Republics of South Africa and Eire.
All Rights Reserved. International Copyright Secured.

Comp 1.

Dean.

Ballad Style — Slow Romantic Song, Calm Relaxing Mood.

Bassline — Copy from Killing Me Softly.

Base Melody around chords of KMS.

But change round to develop into your own song.

House

Since the mid 1980s, house music has established itself as the dominant form of dance music internationally. It is music programmed by humans using computer-based sequencers and electronic sound sources which take out the labour intensive use of musicians. This increasing reliance on technology reflects the changes that took place within many industries throughout the 80s and 90s. Because new technology has lessened the costs of producing records in real terms, record companies can now afford to target different sectors of the market with remixes, rather like marketing different flavours of the same crisp.

The roots of house lie in the rhythms and culture of disco. But in clubs such as Chicago's Warehouse (from which the term 'house' is taken), DJ Larry Levan would also play the minimalist euro dance beats of Kraftwerk, the synth pop of British acts such as Soft Cell and Depeche Mode, the synth based euro disco of Giorgio Moroder's productions and even punk tracks to a crowd that crossed the boundaries of race and sexuality.

The tune that lays claim to be the first house track was 'Fantasy' by Jessie Saunders, a mixture of synthetic strings, a Moroder style bass line and a drum machine beat. A party scene started to develop and the DJs associated with it: Ron Hardy, Farley 'Jackmaster' Funk and the 'Hot Mix 5', started DJing on the radio, spreading the new sounds as well as recording rhythm 'trax' (drum machine beats) for their own use rather than release.

However, with the founding of labels such as Trax Records and DJ International, more musical elements started to creep in. Marshall Jefferson's 1986 classic 'Move Your Body', with its pounding piano part, defined the new sound and became known as the 'house music anthem', achieving club success in the UK as well as the US. The first transatlantic house hit came with Farley 'Jackmaster' Funk's 'Love Can't Turn Around', featuring the ecstatic gospel style vocals of Darryl Pandy. Producer Steve Hurley scored a number one with his production of Jim Silk's 'Jack Your Body' (jacking was the house style of dancing), which started a spate of 'Jack' records.

By 1987 the scene was both developing and spreading internationally. Pop house hits such as MARRS' 'Pump Up The Volume' were all the rage in Britain, and in Detroit three school friends, Juan Atkins, Derrick May and Kevin Saunderson, were experimenting with the harder sounds that would come to define 'techno'. Acid house burst onto the scene in 1988, based around the 'squelching' sound of the Roland TB303 bass line machine. In the UK, acid house became the soundtrack of 'rave' culture: often illegal dance parties with dancers fuelled by the drug Ecstasy.

By the 1990s house music and its many offshoots had become the mainstream of dance pop culture and many non-dance acts had their tracks remixed to cross over to a dance market. In the case of Todd Terry's remix of 'Missing' by singer/songwriters Everything But The Girl, the link with dance culture has revitalised their careers, putting their songs of English suburban angst into a contemporary context.

Two typical house-style repetitive piano riffs. Practise at a slow tempo and count all the semiquavers (sixteenth notes), then build up speed.

MISSING

Words by Tracey Thorn
Music by Ben Watt

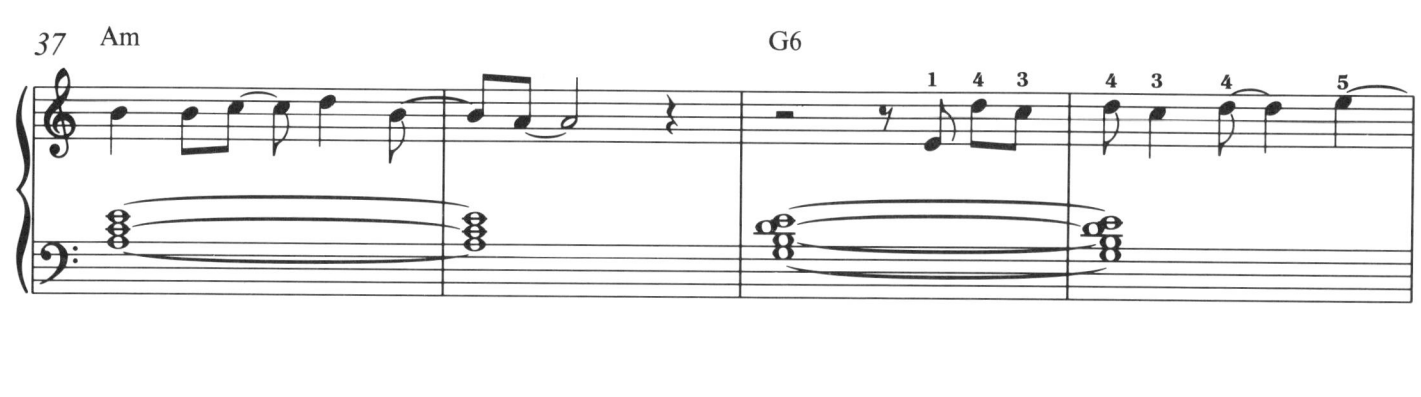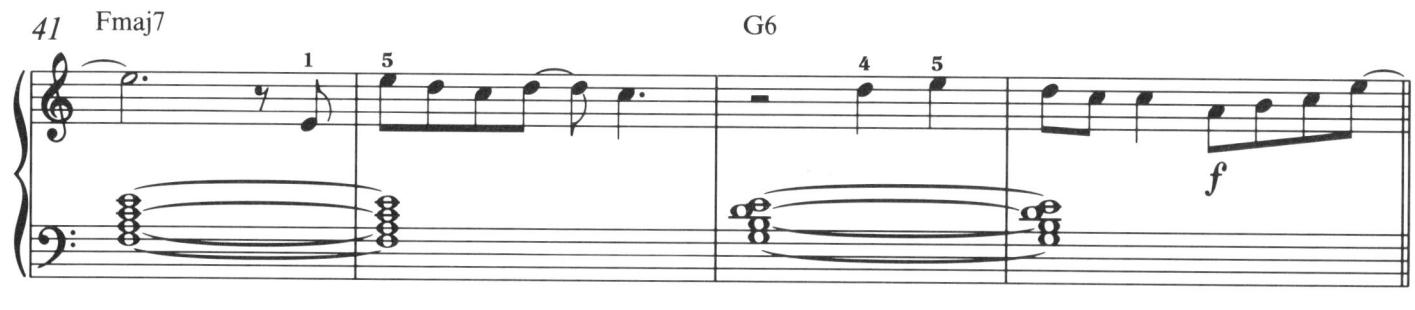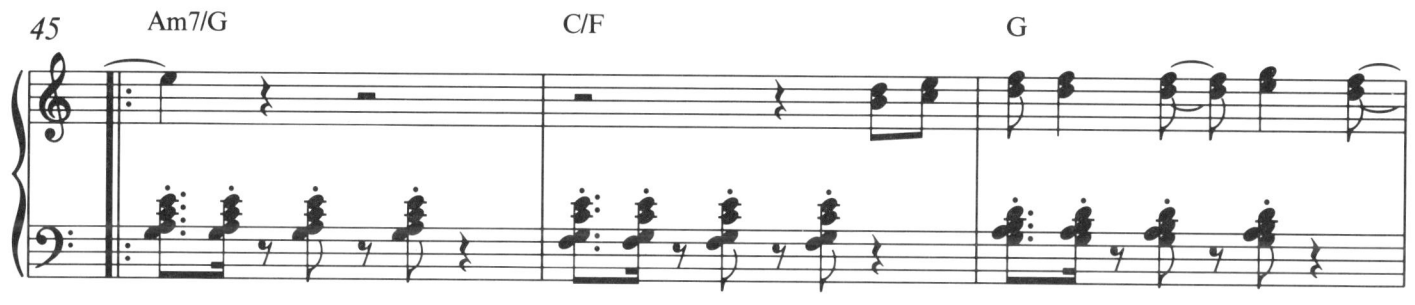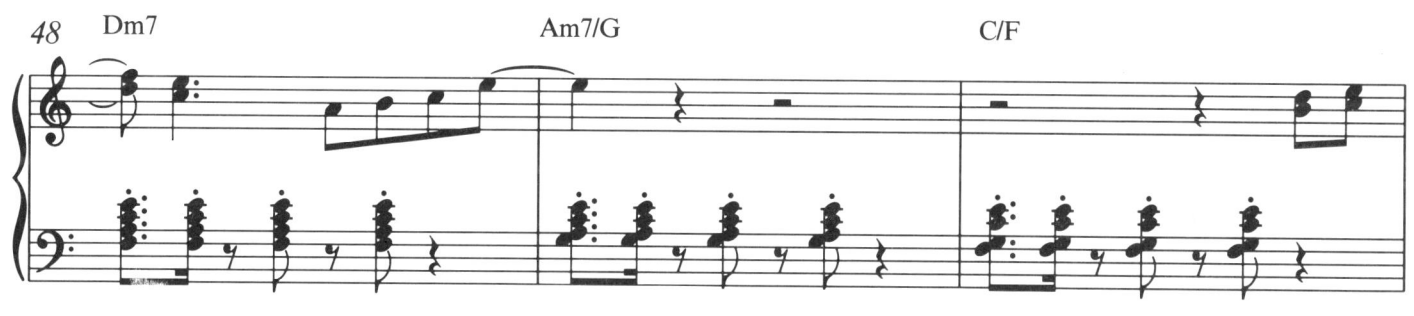

Rhythm & Blues

Rhythm & blues is now used as a blanket term to describe commercial black American pop music ranging from swingbeat to hip-hop, but its roots are in the hard swinging 'jump' groups of the 1940s and 50s. Artists such as Louis Jordan created a trail of influence that can be traced to most areas of pop music today.

One major offshoot is traceable through Jordan's record producer Milt Gabler, who also produced the early white rock 'n' roll tracks for Bill Haley And The Comets. However, the early rock and roll scene had ground to a standstill by the early 1960s: Elvis was in the army, Jerry Lee Lewis was in disgrace for marrying his teenage cousin and Little Richard had turned to the church. But Jordan also influenced the raunchy guitar playing and songs of Chuck Berry, who in turn influenced early British beat groups such as The Beatles, The Rolling Stones and The Who, setting up the British domination of rock in the 60s and 70s.

Another offshoot was reggae, which developed in Jamaica from a combination of New Orleans R & B rhythms and mento, (a Jamaican folk song form). In New York in the late 1960s Latin mambo rhythms crossed with R & B to create the short lived 'boogaloo' dance craze.

The most direct line, however, can be seen in the careers of the artists who started off playing R & B and went on to develop new forms of rhythmic dance music. One such band is the Bar-Kays, who started their career as the second string Stax Records' house band, backing great soul/R & B artists such as Otis Redding and Sam and Dave. Tragedy struck in the form of a plane crash that killed most of the band members as well as Redding, but the band reformed as a Sly And The Family Stone style funk band and then continued to follow trends for over thirty years.

The man who orchestrated the transition from rhythm & blues to funk (leading on to disco, house, swingbeat and hip-hop) was James Brown. Born in South Carolina in 1933 he grew up with his Aunt 'Honey', who ran a brothel and sold illegal liquor. As a teenager he was obsessed by music and sport, he would sweep the floor of the local church to be able to practise the piano, but ended up in jail by his fifteenth birthday.

As with the great jazz innovator Louis Armstrong it was those years 'inside' which allowed him to develop his musicianship, and he formed a gospel choir, the Famous Flames, which started to build a reputation outside the jail once he was released. After seeing a rhythm & blues show featuring big stars such as Hank Ballard and Fats Domino they started to incorporate secular material in their act. The first single 'Please, Please, Please' became a hit on the back of constant touring and the electrically exciting live act. The group changed its name to James Brown And The Famous Flames and took over Little Richard's bookings when he retired from showbusiness. In 1962 they recorded the seminal 'Live At The Apollo' album, which captures the last years of rhythm & blues before Brown moved into funk.

'I Feel Good' is a classic Brown tune of this era which prefigures the funky feels of the following years. Despite recently being imprisoned again Brown continues to work and has scored 114 entries on the Billboard R & B charts and nearly 100 entries on the American Hot 100 singles chart.

I GOT YOU (I FEEL GOOD)

Words & Music by James Brown

© Copyright 1966 Fort Knox Music Co Inc, USA.
Lark Music Limited, Iron Bridge House, 3 Bridge Approach, London NW1 8BD
for the Commonwealth of Nations (excluding Canada/Australasia), Eire and Israel.
All Rights Reserved. International Copyright Secured.

Garage

On a summer's night in 1979 in Comiskey Park in Chicago, a local rock DJ called Steve Dahl started a vinyl bonfire, fuelled with records by artists such as Donna Summer and KC And The Sunshine Band, declaring the death of disco. The riot that ensued and the resulting publicity convinced the major record companies to stop investing in dance music and move back to rock. The upshot of this was that the producers and musicians who had been involved in the disco scene either had to go back underground to the club scene or else cross over into other musical genres. So while Chic founder Nile Rodgers was having tremendous commercial success producing lightweight dance/pop for Madonna ('Like A Virgin') and rock/dance crossover for David Bowie ('Let's Dance'), many of the DJs and producers were starting to manufacture new offshoots of disco on small labels using electronics (synthesisers and drum machines) rather than 'expensive' musicians to create their music.

Two major scenes started to emerge from the ashes of disco: the 'house' scene of Chicago, based around the Warehouse club and DJ Frankie Knuckles, and the 'garage' scene of New York which was also focused on a club, the Paradise Garage, and DJ Larry Levan. As Chicago house was influenced by New York disco, so garage sprang from the early Chicago house music, closing the circle. But despite the similarities, there were also differences between the two styles. Garage would often feature gospel/soul vocals and the tracks would be between five and ten beats per minute slower than the 125 bpm 'jack your body' house style.

In 1984, cult disco DJ Walter Gibbons released a remix of a track called 'Set It Off' under the name of Strafe, which started the transition from disco to garage. It was soon to be followed by the Peech Boys' 'Don't Make Me Wait' and D-Train's 'You're The One For Me'. This was a more minimal, harder, more European sound than the disco product of labels such as Salsoul and Philadelphia International. The track that is considered by many to be the first garage record proper is Paul Scott's 'Off The Wall', released in 1985 and combining a deep soulful feel with a hard edged club beat. By the late 1980s the US garage scene was taking off internationally, with a new generation of divas such as Adeva, whose 1988 cover of Aretha Franklin's soul classic 'Respect' was an international hit.

Top garage remixer Tony Humphries was based close by at the Zanzibar Club in Newark, New Jersey, as well as DJing at New York's Kiss FM radio station. His arrival in the UK coincided with the international success of the UK scene and clubs such as The Hacienda in Manchester and The Ministry Of Sound in London provided a strong launchpad for locally produced dance music. British dance diva Alison Limerick's hit 'Where Love Lives' is a classic slice of garage, with its infectious piano introduction, soulful vocals and pumping bassline.

Start practising this typical house/garage piano groove at a slow tempo and build up the speed until you reach 120 beats per minute.

WHERE LOVE LIVES

Words & Music by Lars Kronlund

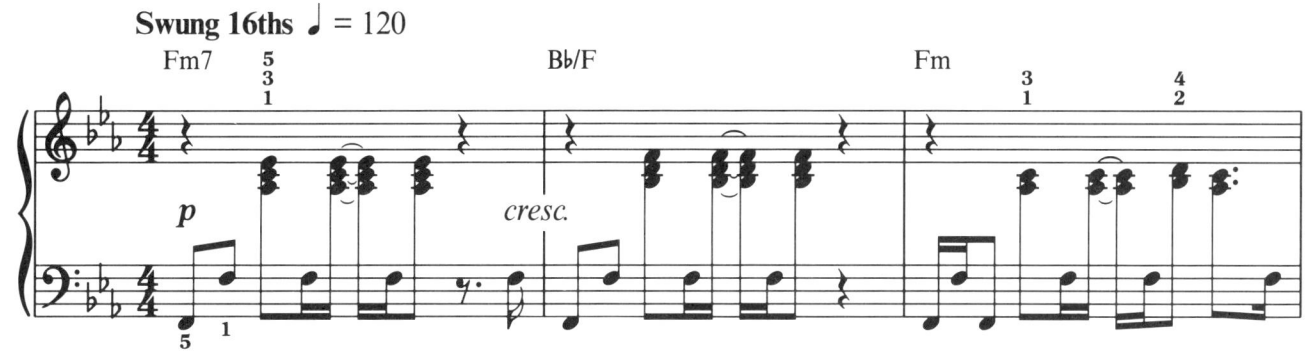
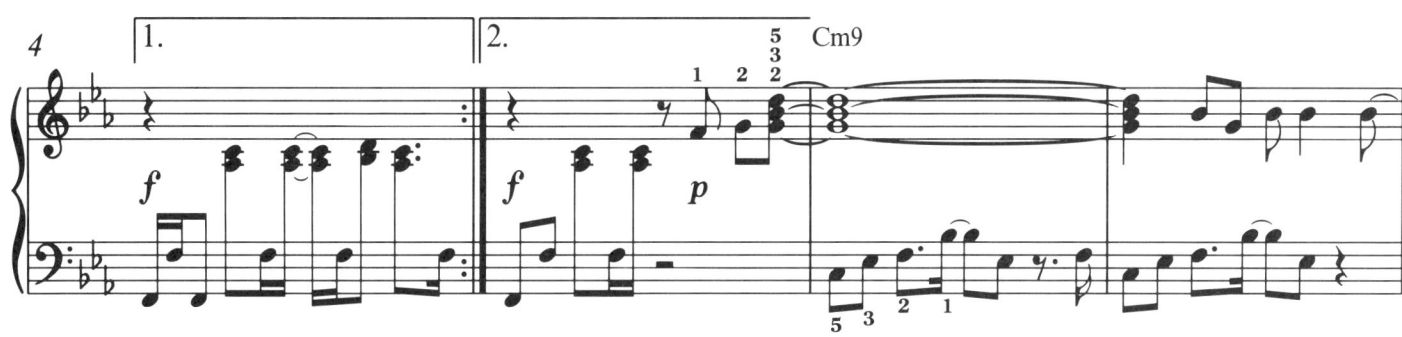

© Copyright 1991 BMG Music Publishing Limited, 69-79 Fulham High Street, London SW6.
This arrangement © Copyright 1997 BMG Music Publishing Limited.
All Rights Reserved. International Copyright Secured.

New Jack Swing/Swingbeat

As rap has moved from the 'old school' sound through hardcore to the celebration of gang life in 'gangsta rap', on the other side of the rhythm and blues tracks is a world where love and passion meets raw sexuality, and the domestic realities of contemporary Afro-American sexual politics are put to song. It is a world which looks back and hears in its parents' record collections an authentic voice of soul and struggle which it tries to recreate for the modern age; but it is also the world of corporate America which has learned to package 'attitude' and sexuality to successive generations of teenagers as adeptly as it once packaged the latest dance craze.

As a distinct Afro-American cultural identity has developed, there has risen the need for role models and in the music business this means pop stars. The roots of the present explosion of black pop music go back to 1983, when the teen group New Edition was formed by black music entrepreneur Maurice Starr as an 80s version of The Jackson 5.

New Edition was the springboard from which some of the major players in the contemporary scene have emerged. Its members included Bobby Brown, Michael Bivins, Ralph Tresvant and Johnny Gill, all of whom have had considerable success. However, it was when Bobby Brown left New Edition in 1987 and teamed up with hot young producer Teddy Riley to produce the massive hit 'My Prerogative' that the floodgates opened to new talent. Riley's 'New Jack Swing' sound: hard swinging, up tempo drum machine grooves combined with multi-layered synthesiser rhythm and melody parts, took over the R & B charts, and the hits kept coming for Riley and his acts such as Keith Sweat, Al B. Sure!, Heavy D and his own group Guy.

The two production teams which had previously dominated the charts, Jimmy Jam and Terry Lewis (Flyte Time Productions) and L.A. Reid and Babyface, picked up on the new grooves and were soon giving Riley a run for his money. Jam and Lewis continued to score hit after hit with acts as varied as Janet Jackson, Johnny Gill, Karyn White, Alexander O'Neal, Ralph Tresvant and the gospel choir The Sounds Of Blackness. They were also involved in the production of the 1990 multi-platinum album Poison by the group Bell Biv Devoe, formed out of the three remaining members of New Edition.

Michael Bivins described the 'swingbeat sound' of the album as being 'smoothed out on the R & B tip with a pop feel to it.' This is the sound that has been at the forefront of black pop in the 1990s. The productions and songs of Riley, Jam and Lewis, L.A. and Babyface and other producers such as Sean 'Puffy' Coombs, fill the records of artists such as R. Kelly, Mary J. Blige, Blackstreet, TLC, En Vogue and those successors to the great Motown vocal groups of the 60s and 70s: Boyz 2 Men, Jodeci and Another Bad Creation.

MY PREROGATIVE

Words & Music by Teddy Riley,
Gene Griffin & Bobby Brown

Calypso/Soca

As with the blues in the southern states of the USA, the roots of Trinidadian calypso come from West Africa. Slaves were sent from Africa to the Caribbean where they continued the tradition of the 'Griot': the tribal folklorist and storyteller. By the start of the 20th century their songs of social comment or protest were known as 'calipsos' and it became usual for audiences to shout 'Kaiso', a West African Hausa word meaning 'bravo', during their performance.

Calypso rhythms and melodies show a strong African influence, with a hint of Trinidad's near neighbour Venezuela, in the melody. The harmony is usually diatonic (melodies and chords deriving from the major scale of the tonic key) and there is a highly distinctive and syncopated rhythmic approach to melody.

In 1838 the slave apprenticeships ended in Trinidad and this meant that the Trinidad carnival stopped being a genteel affair with costumed/masquerade bands and returned to its African roots. Costumed/masquerade bands would practise for the carnival in tents in the capital Port of Spain, and in 1921 'Chieftain' Walter Douglas started charging for entry to the tents. Calypso shows are still known as 'tents'.

Calypso started to be recorded in 1914 when American record company Victor came to the island, and in the same year the first national calypso contest was held. In 1939 this became the Calypso King (now Monarch) competition, where seven contestants compete against the reigning 'king'. The contestants have to perform two songs each, one serious and one light-hearted. Great calypso names include Attila The Hun, Growling Tiger and The Mighty Sparrow.

Soca is a more commercial form of calypso, its name coming from the first and last two letters of calypso. It was developed in 1973 by calypsonian King Ras Shorty 1st in his tune 'Endless Vibrations' to safeguard the calypso tradition against the rival attractions of Jamaican reggae. It features a highly rhythmic bassline compared to calypso as well as syncopated brass, guitar and percussion parts. Mighty Arrow's 'Hot, Hot, Hot' shot the genre to fame when it became an international hit and it is a classic example of a 'party' soca tune.

A typical calypso rhythm:

HOT, HOT, HOT

Words & Music by Alphonsus Cassell

Acid Jazz

In some ways it is easier to describe what 'acid jazz' isn't. The term is used as a catch-all to describe an area of dance music that is not one of the offshoots of disco, house or techno and doesn't fit into the mainstream of contemporary rhythm and blues. It does look to 70s' funk, 60s' soul/jazz, Latin and hip-hop for inspiration, with different artists creating their own synthesis of these elements.

You may well hear Latin percussion, Fender Rhodes or Wurlitzer electric piano, Jimmy Smith-inspired Hammond B3 organ playing, Stevie Wonder-style clavinet and Herbie Hancock-style analogue synth lines. Or perhaps 70s' wah-wah guitar or George Benson jazz-funk guitar licks, Roy Ayers-style vibraphone and underpinning it all a funky drum groove – either a 70s style 'rare groove' or a 'fat' hip-hop beat.

As legend has it the phrase 'acid jazz' was first used by DJ Gilles Peterson who was the leading figure in the booming jazz dance scene in London in the mid 1980s. The story goes that he was taking over from an 'acid house' DJ at a club and to try to keep the dancers on the dancefloor introduced his collection of hard bop, soul jazz and rare grooves as 'acid jazz', and the phrase stuck.

Peterson went on to run the legendary 'Talkin' Loud' sessions at Dingwalls in Camden Lock. These Sunday lunch jam sessions would bring together jazz dancers and musicians, rappers and refugees from the jazz-funk scene, creating a mix of music, style and attitude which Peterson recreated in the formation of two record labels, firstly Acid Jazz with partner Eddie Piller, and then the Polygram funded Talkin' Loud.

The mix of hip-hop and jazz that we now take for granted only started to make its presence felt at the beginning of the 90s. New York hip-hop outfit Gangstarr hooked up with young sax virtuoso Branford Marsalis to create 'Jazz Thing', the lead track from Spike Lee's jazz film Mo' Better Blues. Miles Davis lent his authority to this new fusion with 'Doo-Bop', his last, posthumously released album and in 1992 British jazz guitarist Ronny Jordan achieved both chart success and dancefloor credibility with his version of Miles Davis' 'So What'.

Acid jazz can never be any one thing and it has been reinvented for domestic consumption in all the different countries the scene has spread to. But if you find your foot tapping to Branford Marsalis' 'Buckshot LeFonque' or the Blue Note label jazz sampling of US 3, the Stevie Wonder influenced funk of Jamiroquai, the contemporary jazz-funk of Incognito, the 'Tower Of Power' style funk of The Brand New Heavies, the Hammond Organ lead soul jazz of the James Taylor Quartet or the rap and reggae influenced jazz-funk of Galliano, you can be sure that someone somewhere is calling it 'acid jazz'.

Try this Miles Davis style riff over a D minor funky groove. The bottom four notes in this voicing are a fourth apart, which sounds quite different to the usual triadic based chords.

APPARENTLY NOTHIN'

Words & Music by Carleen Anderson & Marco Nelson

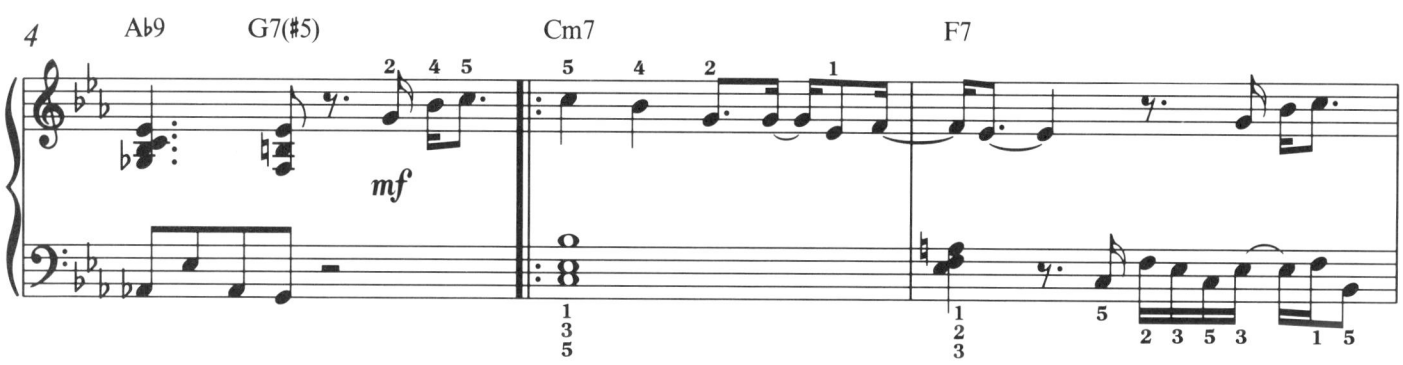
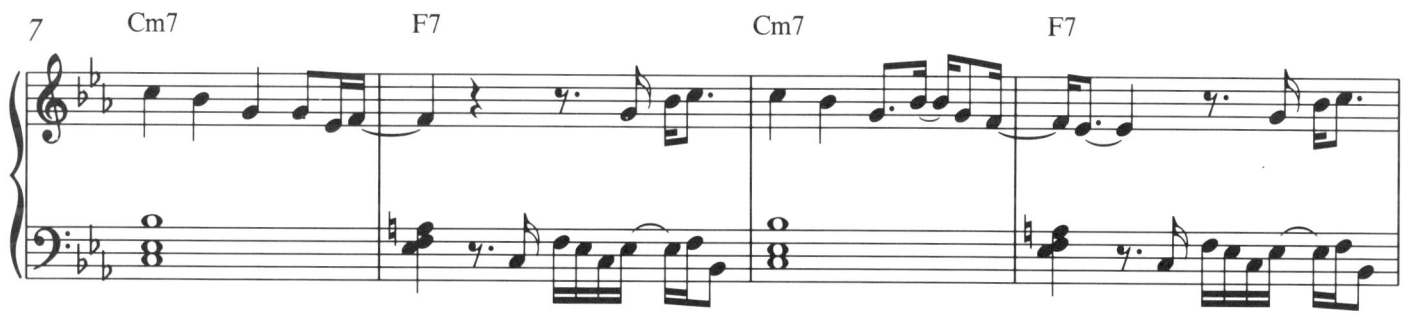

© Copyright 1991 MCA Music Limited, 77 Fulham Palace Road, London W6.
All Rights Reserved. International Copyright Secured.

Funk

When black entrepreneur Berry Gordy set up Motown records in the early 1960s he was more interested in selling records than in promoting a black civil rights agenda. But the success that he had (with artists such as Stevie Wonder, Diana Ross and Marvin Gaye) may have achieved more for 'black consciousness' than any political movement. Motown's achievement was to bring black pop music and artists into the mainstream by tailoring black music for white audiences. However, with the rise of the black power movement it was clear that both black and white audiences were ready for music which made no concessions to colour in its pursuit of the perfect dance groove.

The term 'funk' originally meant dirty or bad smelling. In the early 1950s it was used to describe the post-cool school jazz of pianists such as Horace Silver and Herbie Hancock, with the return to harder swinging and bluesy feels. However, the key figure in the transition from the rhythm and blues of the late 50s/early 60s to funk was James Brown.

From his 1956 hit, 'Please, Please, Please', Brown dominated the Rhythm and Blues charts in the USA until the mid 70s. But it was with the release of his 1965 hit 'Papa's Got A Brand New Bag' that he created the rhythmic changes within rhythm and blues which became 'funk'. This was done by shifting the rhythmic emphasis from beats two and four to beats one and three, as in rock. Syncopated, swung semiquaver (16th note) rhythms or melodies would be played against this. This formula proved very popular and Brown combined it with imagery of black assertiveness in tracks such as 'Say It Loud, I'm Black And I'm Proud' (1968).

The spark that Brown had lit has gone on to influence nearly every area of popular music, from jazz keyboard players (such as George Duke, Herbie Hancock and Weather Report's Joe Zawinul) to rock (Rick James and Prince combined the two genres most effectively). Funk rhythms laid the foundations for 'Philadelphia Soul', which turned into disco, which mutated into house, out of which came techno, and so on. Funk has also provided the basis for hip-hop and swingbeat, and many of Brown's tracks have been sampled for use in hip-hop tracks. His best known recording was the 1970 classic 'Get Up I Feel Like Being A Sex Machine', propelled by the elastic bass of the young Bootsy Collins and featuring a minimalistic piano solo against a sparse funk backdrop which prefigures much of the 'street soul' sounds of the early 90s.

The other great funk innovator was Sly Stone and his group Sly And The Family Stone. Based in the flower power atmosphere of San Francisco in the late 1960s, they fused funk rhythms, propelled by the innovative 'slap' bass style of Larry Graham, with the textures of psychedelic rock. Their multi-racial/gender line-up and messages of unity in hits such as 'Dance To The Music' and 'Family Affair' struck a chord in a country riven by deep racial divisions.

The great funk keyboard players such as Bernie Worrell, Stevie Wonder and Herbie Hancock would use instruments such as Wurlitzer or Fender Rhodes electric pianos, sometimes treated with electronics, the Hohner Clavinet (a keyboard on which each note plucked a string which was then amplified, as featured on Stevie Wonder's seminal 1972 track 'Superstition') and early analogue synthesisers such as the Mini-moog and the ARP 2600.

Scottish funk band Average White Band scored a number one hit in the USA in 1974 with their tune 'Pick Up The Pieces', which has since become a funk classic.

This is a typical 'funky clavinet' feel, using intervals of a fourth around the blues scale.

PICK UP THE PIECES

Music by Roger Ball & Hamish Stuart

© Copyright 1974 Average Music Incorporated, USA.
Island Music Limited, 47 British Grove, London W4.
All Rights Reserved. International Copyright Secured.

Improvise using notes from a) B flat mixolydian scale, major with a flat 7th, or b) the B flat blues scale.

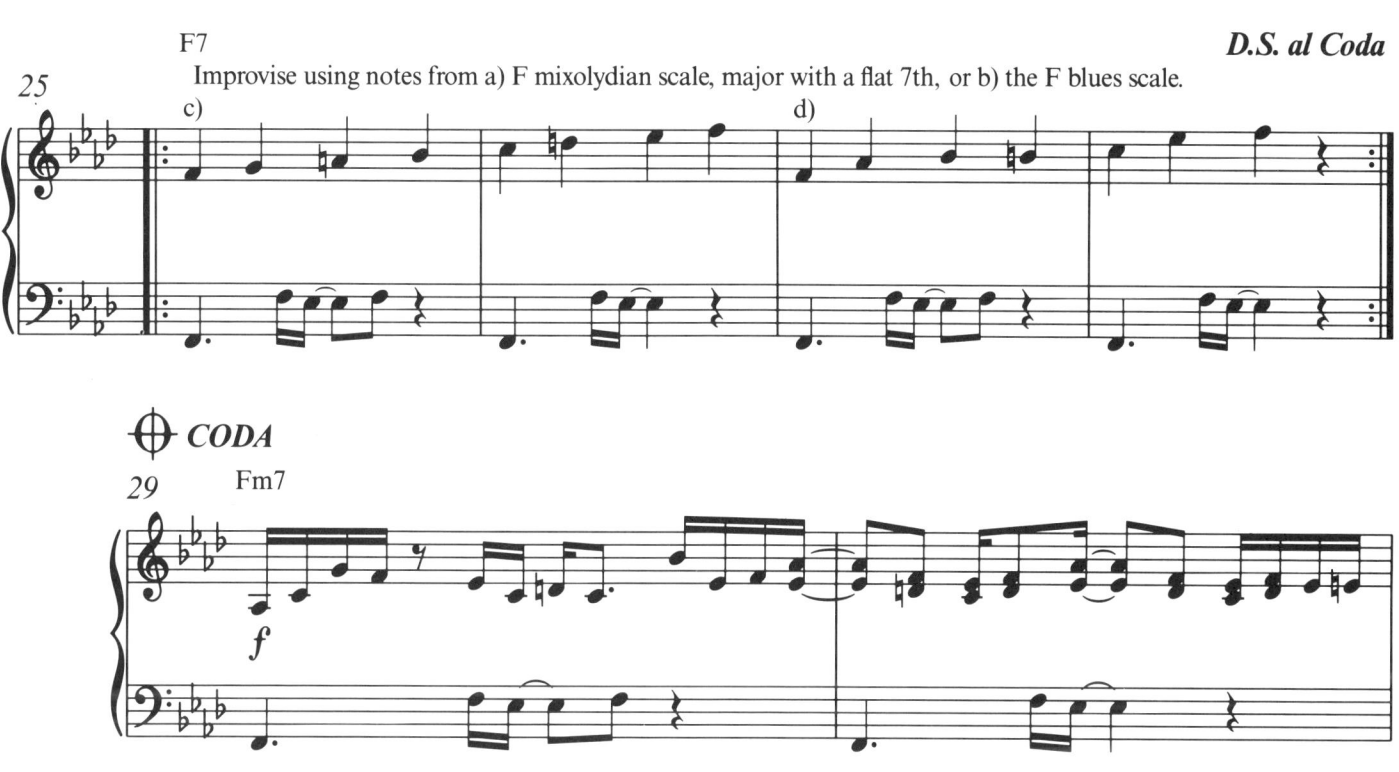

Improvise using notes from a) F mixolydian scale, major with a flat 7th, or b) the F blues scale.

Jazz-Funk

From the late 1950s onwards, progressive jazz artists such as saxophonists John Coltrane and Ornette Coleman were moving further away from the dance roots of jazz to something more spiritual, abstract and 'difficult'. This turning of jazz away from the spectrum of mainstream entertainment into an avant-garde art form created a self-fulfilling prophesy where if the music wasn't 'difficult' it was considered a sell-out to commercialism. But this led to the music becoming a minority interest, running on a low economic level.

For a younger generation of black jazz musicians, who had possibly not suffered to such a degree from racism and were quite often college educated and middle-class, ignoring the mass market did not seem to make sense. They had grown up seeing the success of pop music and the way that rhythm and blues artists such as James Brown and Jimi Hendrix had managed to be both musically innovative and appeal to the mass market. As ever it was Miles Davis who started things off by bringing electric keyboards into jazz in 1969 with his albums 'In A Silent Way' and 'Bitches Brew' and it was Davis' 'alumni' who were at the forefront of developing the funky, electric new sounds.

Pianist/keyboard player Herbie Hancock, who was a key member of Davis' mid 60s' bands, combined funky drum grooves with fat synthesiser bass and lead lines, electric piano and other electric keyboards, electric guitar and brass on his 1973 album 'Headhunters'. Its track 'Chameleon' defined this new jazz-funk sound, an update on the 'funky' jazz of Horace Silver.

Guitarist George Benson side-stepped the jazz world (he turned down an opportunity to join Davis' group) to make a series of classic jazz-funk albums featuring mellow funky workouts of pop songs with his trademark scat vocal/guitar solos. He achieved great commercial success with albums such as 'Breezin'' and his versions of classic songs such as 'On Broadway' and 'This Masquerade'.

The saxophone was at the forefront of this music, with Grover Washington reinventing the sax as a rhythm and blues lead instrument in 'Mr Magic' and in his collaboration with soulful pop singer Bill Withers, 'Just The Two Of Us'.

Jazz-funk offered a cooler, more sophisticated option to musicians and audience looking for a mid point between hardcore disco/funk and the contemporary jazz scene. Weather Report's 'Birdland', featuring the big band influenced synth work of Austrian Joe Zawinul and sax of Wayne Shorter (both ex Davis), crosses over between jazz-funk and jazz-rock and has become one of the few 'standard' tunes coming from the 1970s.

Jazz-funk's legacy has been huge: from acid jazz, influenced by artists such as vibesman Roy Ayers, to 'Quiet Storm', a very popular American radio format consisting of mellow funky grooves with soulful instrumentals or vocals on top, from hip-hop to 80s' fusion. But in a sense it was never any more or less than what Louis Jordan was doing with rhythm and blues in the 1940s – a combination of pop music, dance beats and a jazz influence.

A classic 1970s jazz-funk groove:

BIRDLAND

Music by Josef Zawinul

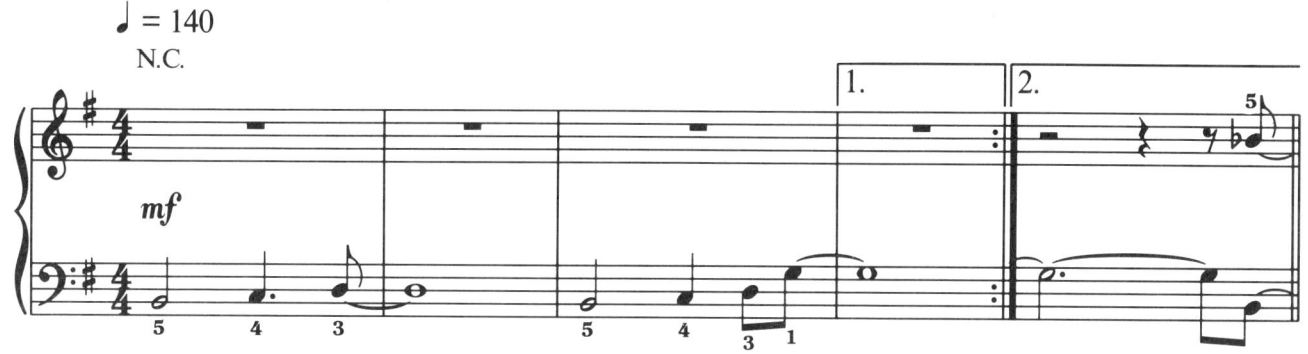

© Copyright 1977, 1978 Mulatto Music, USA.
MCA Music Limited, 77 Fulham Palace Road, London W6.
All Rights Reserved. International Copyright Secured.

Salsa

The word salsa, coming from the Spanish word meaning sauce but also used as slang by Cuban musicians to mean hot, describes a group of up tempo Latin American dance styles and rhythms including the mambo, cha-cha-cha, guaguanco, guijira and merengue. Cuba, like most of the Caribbean, has a racially mixed population – black, white and mulatto – and this mix is reflected in Cuban culture, particularly the music, where there is a coming together of Spanish and African influences.

The roots of salsa go back to the start of the 1900s, with the development in Eastern Cuba of the two-part folksong form, the 'son'. In the 1940s, Perez Prado, a Cuban émigré living in Mexico City, developed the 'mambo', which combined the swinging sounds of the jazz big bands with the rhythms of the Cuban son. The mambo became very popular in New York, with bandleaders such as Machito having great success with bands which integrated jazz soloing with a Latin feel. Be-bop pioneer and trumpeter Dizzy Gillespie, one of the most important jazz musicians of the 1940s, picked up on this Afro-Cuban feel, recognising the African rhythmic roots to be the same as those of jazz. This started a cultural dialogue between North and South American cultures that still goes on today.

Another of the major Latin bandleaders in New York in the 1940s was Puerto Rican percussionist Tito Puente. There have always been close cultural links between Cuba and Puerto Rico, which also has its own dance forms such as the 'bomba', but from the 1920s onwards Puerto Rican culture developed not only on the island itself, but also in New York city. This large community became involved not just in the salsa scene of the 70s, but also in the early disco scene and now in the 'Nuyorican' scene – a mix of contemporary house based dance sounds and Latin music.

Dominican bandleader Johnny Pacheco founded the Fania label in the 70s and he used the word salsa as a marketing tool to sell up tempo Latin dance music. This scene became very successful with bandleaders such as Willie Colon selling records all over the Spanish speaking world. Colon featured singers like the innovative Ruben Blades in his band, who sang tales about the inhabitants of 'El Barrio', the Latin-American ghetto in Harlem.

As the salsa boom died down and the next Latin craze took over (the merengue), salsa reinvented itself as salsa romantica, a slicker version of itself sung by handsome white 'pop stars'. However, it took until the late 1980s for salsa to make an impact on the traditionally conservative North American public.

The artist who achieved this was Gloria Estefan. Born in Cuba, her family moved to Miami when she was young, where she met and married her husband Emilio. He persuaded her to join his band, which eventually became The Miami Sound Machine. After several Latin inflected disco hits in the UK and Spanish speaking markets, Gloria broke through in the USA with the English language album 'Primitive Love Breakthrough'. She has now also had successful pop hits recorded solely in Spanish, and the international hit 'Oye Mi Canto' (Hear My Voice) is a marvellous introduction to exciting Latin piano playing. The 'montuno' style (which is featured in 'Oye Mi Canto' where the solo piano plays a repetitive syncopated rhythmic part based on arpeggios) can also be heard in recordings by Latin piano pioneers such as the great Eddie Palmieri.

'Montuno' style passage in 'Oye Mi Canto'. Practise it slowly at first, making sure all the syncopations are correct.

OYE MI CANTO (HEAR MY VOICE)

Words by Gloria Estefan
Music by Gloria Estefan, Jorge Casas & Cley Ostwald

© Copyright 1989 Foreign Imported Productions & Publishing Incorporated/Estefan Music Publishing Incorporated, USA.
Assigned to EMI Songs Limited, 127 Charing Cross Road, London WC2.
All Rights Reserved. International Copyright Secured.

Disco

The early 1970s saw a revival in New York of clubs featuring dance-orientated black pop records. This 'disco' scene (derived from the French *discothèque*, meaning record library) had its roots in the early 1960s, when bars and taverns had juke boxes installed and were marketed as discos, featuring the music of the dance craze of that period, the ubiquitous 'Twist'. However, whilst the Twist and the other dance crazes that came in its wake were firmly in mainstream pop culture, the nascent disco scene was much more underground and localised. It catered for a primarily gay, black and Hispanic audience who, fuelled on a cocktail of drugs, celebrated the hedonism of the pre Aids, post Stonewall gay scene.

The undisputed stars of this pleasure seeking subculture were the DJs who plied their trade in the clubs and lofts of New York, developing new mixing techniques and sound systems to cater for the new dance music. These DJs, such as Francis Grasso who worked at The Salvation and David Mancuso at The Loft, lit a spark which eventually turned into the worldwide commercial disco explosion that took place after the release of the movie Saturday Night Fever in 1977 (starring John Travolta and with music by The Bee Gees). They also created a mix of urban dance music, drugs and pleasure seeking that has since been repeated through the 1980s and 90s in the house music scene.

The music played in the clubs was a mix of James Brown-style funk, lushly orchestrated 'Philadelphia Soul' and percussion driven instrumentals as on African émigré Manu Dibango's 'Soul Makossa'. The chart success of 'Soul Makossa' in 1973 made record companies realise that success in the clubs could be a route to airplay on AM (pop) radio. Many dance-based hits followed this trend: George McCrae's 'Rock Your Baby', Barry White's 'You're My First, My Last, My Everything' and The Hues Corporation's 'Rock The Boat'.

However, after Saturday Night Fever was released, disco took over the US single charts. The soundtrack album, with hits such as The Bee Gees' 'Stayin' Alive' and 'Night Fever', was a huge international success and 'disco culture' swept over the whole world. Dance schools were full of aspiring John Travoltas learning the steps to 'the Hustle' – the primary disco dance step. Celebrities thronged to be seen at Studio 54, New York's premier disco club and soon there were even roller (as in roller-skating) discos. Saturday Night Fever made disco safe for the suburban white audience, taking it away from its gay, black and druggy roots and turning it into a glamorous and aspirational parable of the American dream.

The musical content of disco centres around a repetitive drum/percussion pattern, often with 4 bass drum beats to the bar and offbeat hihat skips, rather like the programmed beats of house music in the 80s and 90s. The Bee Gees were the first group to use drum loops – literally loops of recording tape with a drum beat on – to keep a constant groove throughout the whole tune (the same loop was used on several of their hits, being played at differing speeds on each track). In 1975, a DJ called Tom Moulton did the first 12 inch extended remix. Not only was the audio quality better on 12 inches of vinyl as opposed to the usual 7 inches, but it allowed DJs to extend tracks, breaking them down to their percussive essentials and then building them up again.

Disco fell out of favour in the early 80s, but it remains an enormously influential genre, inspiring many artists throughout the 80s and 90s. Synthesisers were introduced to disco music by European producer Giorgio Moroder on Donna Summer's 'I Feel Love', and the throbbing bass synth feel of this track influenced many of the British synth pop and New Romantic bands of the early 80s.

The undisputed 'Queen of Disco', Gloria Gaynor first charted in 1974 with a cover version of a Jackson 5 tune, 'Never Can Say Goodbye', but her treatment of her 1979 no.1 pop hit 'I Will Survive', with its slow piano introduction and swirling orchestral violins, created a dancefloor anthem of personal liberation, its central message still affecting listeners today.

I WILL SURVIVE

Words & Music by Dino Fekaris & Freddie Perren

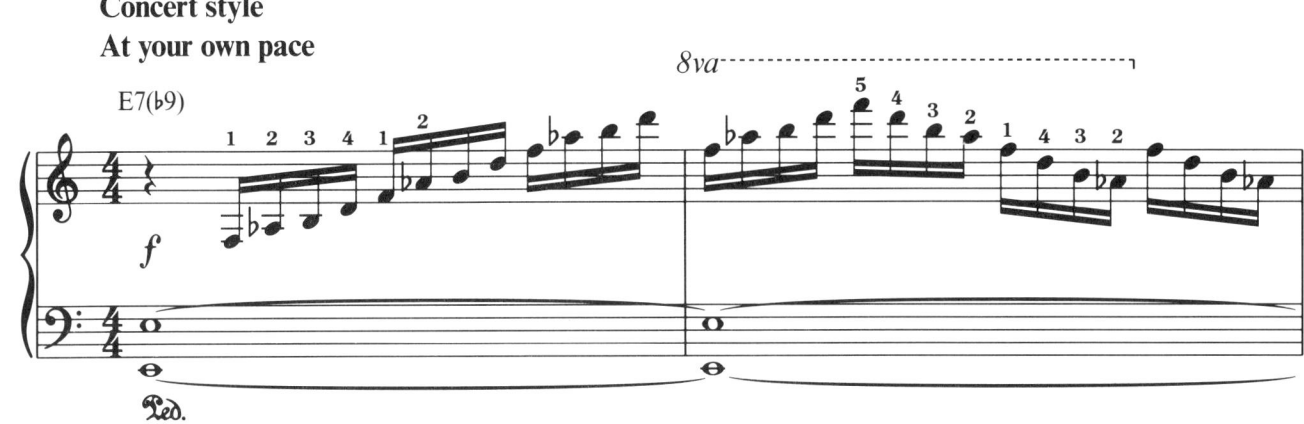

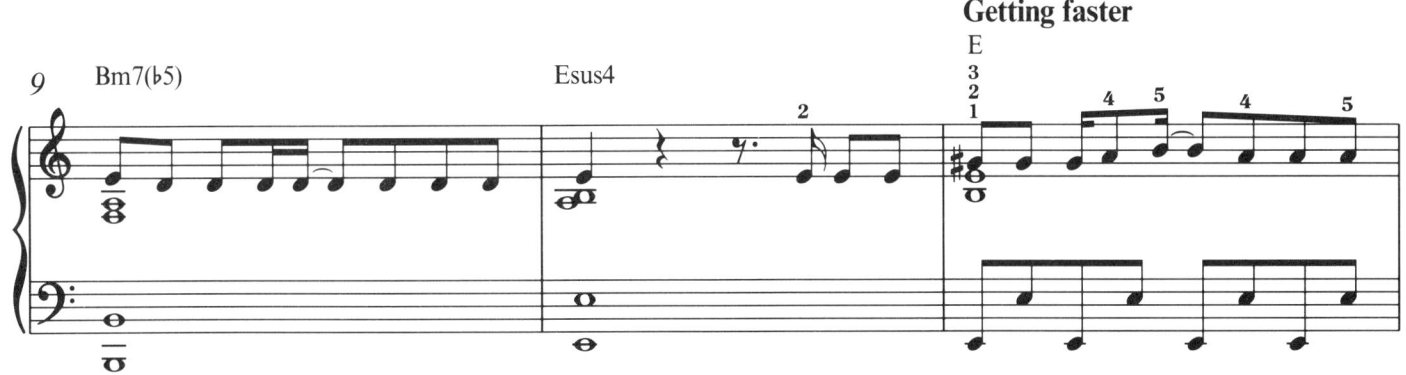

© Copyright 1978 Perren-Vibes Music & PolyGram International Publishing Incorporated, USA for the World.
PolyGram Music Publishing Limited, 47 British Grove, London W4.
All Rights Reserved. International Copyright Secured.